Does the Church Really Have Good News?

5 Promises

✞

David May

DEDICATION

I am dedicating this one to all the good people who have passed through the Santo Guest House. They have come to build buildings and to build lives. They have taught children and they have taught children's teachers. They have painted orphanages and have bought and issued meds. They have learned the language and have dreamed dreams together. They have come from the north and from the south, but they have all come because they love people and they want to help. And whatever else they did here, they have spread good news throughout the land. The people of Haiti are glad they have been here. Thank you to each one.

It is also dedicated to the truth seekers who will pick it up, look it over and give it some serious consideration. It doesn't answer all your questions, but maybe it will help as you continue to seek.

ACKNOWLEDGMENTS

Again I acknowledge the help and advice of Charlene, my wife of 48 years. And all those who have passed through my life who continue to point me toward seeing things as God sees them - who seem to remember the good things Jesus said about the kingdom and don't get all tangled up in the bad stuff that happens in this world. Thanks for maintaining my perspective. In this regard, I especially acknowledge the men who faithfully attend the Eagan men's Bible study group and are so encouraging every other Saturday morning. And, finally, that small handful of people who have really liked my other three books and who have encouraged me to keep writing. Thanks gang.

CONTENTS

– Part 1 –

INTRODUCTION

1

Good News?

Did anyone ever tell you they have good news then proceed to tell you how to escape some horrible fate you didn't believe was real? It's like, "Hey Buddy, you have this horrible disease and I can sell you this really expensive cure. You got a minute?" But you feel great and don't have the time.

That is the way a lot of Christians come on. They think they have good news, but it turns out to be about escaping some horrible fate after death that sounds a little farfetched to you. It is "religious stuff" and you have to be a believer for it to make sense.

But this little book is about some really good news that often gets overlooked in the Christian sales pitch. It is about five important promises that have been made to all of us by someone who is able to keep them and who has a looooong track record of doing so:

1. There is nothing you need to worry about;
2. There is nothing in this world you need to be afraid of;

3.   You don't even need to be concerned about dying;
4.   You are being invited into a family whose logo is that we love each other; and
5.   This world is not your home.

Sounds eerie, doesn't it. Is this just more religious mumbo-jumbo? By my own experience and that of others I know, I can say it is not. Everyone believes something about how this world works. I am just asking that you spend a few minutes looking at how I see it.

In Chapter 10 we will get into what we know about what happens after you die and about why you do not need to be afraid of that. Before that we will look into each of the five bits of good news listed above. But first we need to consider some basic facts that I think we can agree on.

– Part 2 –
SOME PRELIMINARIES

2
God and Science

This may come as a surprise. God is not anti-science. Science is the systematic discovery of truth. God is the original source of truth. There is no conflict. Where the two get at odds is where God's believers get a model fixed in their heads that is contrary to truth (say that the world is flat) and just will not let go in the face of growing evidence to the contrary. Read this next sentence twice. God didn't tell us things that he intended us to interpret in ways that are contrary to compelling scientific evidence.

Another way that science and God come to be at odds is when scientists form a conclusion that is not adequately supported by the evidence. Sometimes they will take a few data points and draw a trend line much farther into the future than their data can really support. Or they will come up with a theory and collect data to support it, ignoring data that would refute it. You see, scientists and Christians are both people and are both subject to letting their desire to be right and to win the argument get in the way of an honest search for the truth.

False Dichotomies

"The traffic light was either red or it was green. Which was it?"

"Well, sir, the traffic light was not working. It was neither red nor green." Or, "No, sir, it was neither; it was yellow." The "red or green" assertion is a rather simple example of what is called a "false dichotomy."

A false dichotomy is an assertion that one of two opposing statements has to be true. Both religious people and scientists sometime lay out false dichotomies either out of ignorance or in an attempt to win the argument. Sometimes they even agree on the false dichotomy, but disagree on the conclusions they draw from it. For example: "There can't be any such thing as evolution because the Bible says God created the earth in seven days." Either God created the world, or the theory of evolution is true. Yet we know that species change to meet the demands of their environments. The false dichotomy says that one or the other must be true, when it is possible (likely even) that God built into his creation the ability for species to adapt to their environments.

Or try this one. "God can't be good if bad things happen to good people." That is another false dichotomy. Either God is good, or bad things happen to good people; both cannot be true. But both can be, and are, true. The dichotomy ignores the fact that in his goodness, God has given us free will. He has taken a hands off approach to what many of us choose to do. It also ignores the superior perspective God has of the world in which he sees all time at the same time. What we see as bad for us right now, he may see as a necessary step toward something really cool down the road. More on this later.

So when you are reading arguments from either side, be alert for false dichotomies. Anytime anyone says, "It has to be either A or B" look for the other possibilities, like A and B, or C or D, and you may be able to solve the puzzle for them. But don't expect any accolades. True believers do not like thinkers coming along and busting their bubbles.

3

The Origins Argument

Why do we have to argue about the origins of stuff? Okay I do know about the seven day story in the beginning of the Bible and how a lot of people (including a lot of Christians) have trouble with that.

Here's how I figure that. If God made a tree on the third day and it was immediately cut down (don't ask who cut it down, just stay with me here), would it have had growth rings? I think so, because that's a part of what trees are.

And if a forester happened by before dark and saw it and you asked him how old it was, he could have told you. He might have said it was seventy or a hundred years old. Would he have been right? In a way, yes, because that's how many rings it had. In another way he would have been wrong because it was just made that morning.

It's a little more complicated with geologic formations and with carbon dating fossils, but the principle is the same. That's not God trying to pull a fast one, that is him just establishing some scientific principles and then being consistent with them.

4

"True Believers"

Science and religion both have their "true believers." "True believers" in this sense are those who will continue to believe what they believe in the face of insurmountable evidence to the contrary. They will not consider that maybe they have seen things through a particular lens and that lens has distorted their vision.

If you approach the existence of matter, and life, and intelligence, and emotions with the notion that there is an all powerful creator of all things, that is where you will find the answers to questions about the source of those things. If you approach them with the assumption that there is no such creator, then you will look for other answers and will often grab onto suggested explanations no matter how absurd they may sound. Your assumptions have a strong influence on your conclusions.

As long as we have had any way of knowing what humankind was thinking we know that they have asked the questions, "Where did we come from?" and "Why are we here?" Some very ancient writers explained it with stories about a creator and claimed they had direct contact with that creator. Some very bright people even today, some of them scientists, believe those stories.

On the other hand there are those, also very bright, people today who laugh at the idea. Often they will point to science and say that it proves that there is no creator. Science doesn't do that and it cannot. You can't prove the non-existence of something you cannot measure by sight, sound, or smell or with the finest of instruments. Some would say that is a convenient argument for those who do believe, and, indeed, it is. But it is what it is, and it cannot be disproved. So, the discussion might as well go in a different direction. Science, again, is a search for truth using the scientific method. You either believe in a creator or you don't. Or you just aren't sure.

If you do believe there was one creator of everything, please be sure that you believe it because you have examined the evidence. If you believe there is no such creator, please be sure it is because you have examined all the evidence and keep your mind open to new facts. If you are uncertain, then I would suggest that the promises we will discuss in the forthcoming chapters make it well worth your efforts to dig into the evidence.

While you are digging, consider the motives of the authors you are reading. Are they "true believers" who present all the evidence on one side of the argument while ignoring facts that would support the other side? If so, weigh their writings accordingly, whether they are religious writers or scientists writing for scientific journals.

5

Is There a "God Particle"?

Since the awarding of the Nobel prizes in 2013, you have probably read about the discovery (or more accurately the evidence of the existence of) what has been called "The God Particle," actually the Higgs Boson. This search and discovery have caused some confusion in the media because of the unfortunate nickname given the particle.

The existence (or non-existence) of the Higgs boson is irrelevant to an understanding of the origin of things. The title, "God Particle" given it to describe its illusiveness was an unfortunate choice of terms. It has been picked up by some of the media as if it were important to the discussion of the existence of a creator. The search is an important one for scientists trying to figure out how the universe works, but whether there is a Higgs Boson or not is irrelevant to the discussion about the existence of God.

Brian Dodson said this about it on July 26, 2012, in "Is it or isn't it? The Higgs boson story" in "Gizmag," an online technology magazine:

"Before we start, let's get rid of one widespread misconception being thrown about by the news media. The Higgs boson is often called the God particle (but never by scientists). The reason for that moniker is that Leon Lederman, Director Emeritus of Fermilab and Nobel Prize winner, wrote a popular book on the Higgs boson. He wanted to call the book "The Goddamn Particle" because of the difficulty and expense of finding the Higgs, but the publisher thought that sales might suffer. The publisher then suggested "The God Particle" as an alternative, to which Lederman eventually acceded. The name is thus a response to a bad joke, rather than an indication of spirituality or divine origin."

And consider this, reported by Nick Thompson, CNN, October 8, 2013:

"'The Higgs boson is the last missing piece of our current understanding of the most fundamental nature of the universe,' Martin Archer, a physicist at Imperial College in London, told CNN."

"'God particle' is a nickname I don't really like," says Archer. "It's nothing to do with religion – the only (theoretical) similarity is you're seeing something that's a field that's everywhere, in all spaces."

Here is what Leon Lederman, the man who gave it the God Particle name wrote about it.[1] It is

_____

1 *The God Particle: If the Universe Is the Answer, What Is the Question?* A 1993 popular science book by Nobel Prize-winning physicist Leon M. Lederman and science writer Dick Teresi.

"so central to the state of physics today, so crucial to our understanding of the structure of matter, yet so elusive, that I have given it a nickname ..."

The effect of the media on public discourse is powerful and sometimes strange. If there is a Higgs boson, that doesn't prove or disprove anything about God any more than finding evidence that living things are made of cells. We accept that they are, yet the discussion continues: Did God create the cells that make up living organisms, or did they evolve? If they evolved, from what? And where did that come from?

6

A Hokey Request

You have heard this one before, but stick with me here. Let's do an exercise. For the sake of understanding my premises, I am asking you to take your disbelief in God or your doubts and put them in a safe container - somewhere where you will know where they are and they will be intact when you go back for them. It will be like playing a pretend game. Pretend with me that there is a God and that the writers of the New Testament really were speaking for Him. That way we can consider each of these five promises.

As we go through these, I will footnote where in the Bible they are found, so you will not have to take my word for it. As for whether you can believe the Bible, I will have more to say at the end of Chapter 8.

– Part 3 –
PROMISES
TO KEEP

7

Promises 1 &2:
There is Nothing in This World to be Afraid of or to Worry About

How do we get past the worry and fear that seem to be so much a part of our lives today? I live in Haiti where for many people there is often cause to worry about whether there will be anything to feed the kids tonight, or whether the thatch roof will stand up to the coming storm. Yet people there seem less worried about what is coming down the road than we do in the states. What is up with that? Whether we worry or not seems to be tied more to how we see the world than to how likely it is that something bad will happen to us.

First you need to understand that God's relationship with his people is like a loving father and his children.[2] People who follow God are called on to trust him.[3]

---

2 1 Corinthians 1:3
3 John 14:

If you do not have a father you can trust, this part may be a little hard for you, but, again, suspend disbelief and just go with me here. We trust him and we love him because we know that he loves us.

Now, in order to accept that, we have to get through the whole "Why do bad things happen to good people and vice versa?" question we raised earlier. My answer (and God's answer) is "They just do."[4]

A lot of bad things happened to Job. He lost his fortune and all his kids, he had boils all over his body, and his wife was encouraging him to curse God and die. His friends kept lecturing him about whatever he had done wrong to bring all this trouble on himself, but Job knew it was not his fault. The friends kept on and eventually Job issued a complaint to God.

God's answer to Job was simple. Essentially he said, "Who are you to question me? Where were you when I created the earth?" And Job said, simply, "Shut my mouth." God does not answer to us. His ideas are not our ideas, his justice not our justice. God sees all of eternity at once and that gives him a totally different perspective on the things that happen in this world. We cannot hope to see things as he sees them.

God promised a lot of great things, and along with those promises, he promised us trouble.[5] The

---

4   Job 40:1-4
5   John 16:33

problem is not that God causes the car wrecks or the sicknesses; it is that he doesn't step in to head them off. When a man in Colorado gets it in his head that he should go into a movie theater and start shooting, God could give him a heart attack on the way and save us a lot of grief, but he doesn't operate that way.

Here is the issue. God doesn't look at the world like we do. We see the world as made of physical stuff. And we see this life as being something we want to hold on to no matter what. To God, on the other hand, 1000 years is as a day.[6] He does not get anxious about what is happening today because he knows what will happen tomorrow.[7] His focus is on eternity and he sees as good anything that will lead us to a good end of it all.

Yes he will answer prayer and sometimes he will give us a "yes" to our requests, but he never promised us a rose garden. He promised us trouble and then he said "Don't let your heart be troubled."[8] See, there is the difference. It is in our hearts. If we choose to follow him, he promised us joy and peace,[9] but not freedom from trouble. Basically he promised us an attitude that will look beyond the

---

6   2 Peter 3:8
7   1 John 3:20
8   John 14:27
9   Galatians 5:22-23

hard times in this world, knowing that this world is not our home.[10]

Part of the problem is that God loves poor people. The whole Bible is full of references to him loving poor people. For example, when Jesus announced the beginning of his ministry, he said he came to bring good news to the poor.[11] And we have fallen for the idea that God promised us riches. To the contrary Jesus told one rich young man to sell everything he had and give it to the poor, [12] and he praised a poor woman for giving away the last cent she had.[13]

We need to be able to relax about our lives. If we can learn to trust God, we can put him in charge of tomorrow. If we still have the same job tomorrow, we will get up and go do the assigned work. But if we don't still have it, we will do something toward the support of ourselves and our families. He said his people's children do not have to beg for bread. That doesn't mean they will all have a free pass to the local Chinese buffet, but they will have something to eat.

David said poetically in the 23rd psalm that our prayer should be that even if God leads us through a valley that is the "shadow of death" we should not be afraid, because God will be there with us. If we are

---

10   Hebrews 11:8-10, 13-16, 32-40

11   Luke 4:18

12   Luke 18:22

13   Luke 21:1-4

aware of his presence and of his love for us, we will not be afraid.

With God in charge of our lives, we don't have to be afraid of anything. But he goes even further than that. He says we don't even have to worry.

We Christians are notorious worriers. Much of my book, "Peace on Earth?"[14] is about what we worry about and what we should do about it. The short answer is we should stop it and trust in God. He promised we don't need to worry[15]. God takes care of wild flowers, and he will take care of us. The Bible says he made us in his image and he loves us most of all.[16] Worry causes us physical problems and doesn't do any good otherwise.

---

14 amazon.com/author/davidmay

15 Matthew 6:25-34. If you are not familiar with this reference, stop and read it. It is much more eloquent than anything I could write about it; and it is Jesus speaking.

16 Genesis 1:26-31

8

Promise #3: You Don't Even Need to be Concerned About Dying

This is the best of all. Jesus promised that for believers he is making a place with him where the creator hangs out.[17]

Many of the fears of this life (and some would argue all of them) are tied up in the fear of dying. A lot of our entertainment is entertaining because it plays on our fear of death. The hero is surely going to die in this scene. But then he is somehow saved. "Whew!" "That was exciting!"

In fact that is what happened in Jesus' story. If you were reading it for the first time, it would be a suspenseful narrative. The hero comes on the scene. The story, like a lot of good novels starts just before his birth. Luke especially tells it pointing out all the things that happen that created a murmur in the community about him. There was the way John the Baptist's birth was predicted to his dad and the

---

17   John 14:1-3

way his dad named him[18]. And there was the bold announcement to the shepherds about Jesus' birth.[19] It will make a fun study to read Luke and pull out all the places that got people to talking and wondering about this Jesus.

And then there is the gradual buildup of mistrust and resentment among his enemies. It starts with curious questions, and because of the answers he gives, the questions turn into challenges and eventually to traps.

Finally his enemies (the antagonists in this story) plot to kill him. And they do. He had been so full of promise! He had made so many promises! And now he is dead!

Now all along Jesus has been dropping hints of what is coming up. And Luke explains some of them for his audience. Many of the hints, though, are quite obscure. That's what we would call foreshadowing. It doesn't take away from the tension building in the story.

We know the story so well that we miss the apprehension and relief that build then dissolve in it. Finally they kill him and his friends go off together to mourn. That is except for his mom and a couple of other loving women. The women are really heroes in this story.

---

18   Luke 1:8-23; 57-66, especially 66
19   Luke 2:8-20

They go out to the tomb to finish getting his body ready for burial and instead of finding him there they meet a stunning young man who utters the four most important words in the Bible. "He is not here!" the man tells them.

And that is the central point. On a Sunday morning Jesus got up and walked out of the grave, proving once and for all that there is nothing in this world we need to be afraid of. He promised we could live with him forever in a beautiful place – a place with no tears and no death.[20] And he proved his power over death by coming back to life. He was resurrected. Not temporarily like Lazarus and the others he raised while he lived here. He was raised from the dead, showed himself to his followers and to several hundred others; then in front of witnesses rose up into the air to go to that place he was building for us. I am guessing it is built by now and is waiting with him for more of us to believe so we can join him there.[21]

It is a fantastic story, yet a true one. The men who wrote this down said they had checked the details. Some of them had been there.[22] Others interviewed witnesses and fact checked the whole account.[23] If it were not true, why would they not have

20 Revelation 21:1-4
21 2 Peter 3:8-9
22 Mark 3:17-18
23 Luke 1:1-4

just gone home and tried to resurrect the businesses they had abandoned? They had nothing to gain by making up such an incredible tale. In fact history says that most of them were persecuted and killed because they stuck to their guns, giving the same account wherever they went. They held on because the story is true. And they were telling it to claim their spot in the wonderful place Jesus has gone to build for all of us.

"Death is swallowed in victory."[24]

---

24   1 Corinthians 15:54

9

Promise 4: You are Being Invited Into a Group Whose Logo is their Love for Each Other and for Outsiders

Wouldn't you like to be part of a group who really put each other's interests ahead of their own? That's who Jesus said his church was.[25] There are really churches like that. You may have to search for them. But that is the kind of church Jesus built and the kind you want to be a part of. If you don't see one close by you have four options:

1. You can drive a long way to find one;
2. Or you can start one;
3. Or you can stay with the one close by and try to change it;
4. Or you can just sit it out and not be a part of a church.

---

25 Acts 2:44-47

I will list some pros and cons for each approach in just a few minutes. But first let's look at the church Jesus designed. He said this about it: "All people will know that you are my followers if you love each other.[26]" Our love for each other is our corporate logo. It lets people know who we are. It tells them we are real.

In the first church everybody shared everything.[27] Today they would be called socialists. They would sell land or anything else they had and give the money to people who needed it.[28] They ate together, sharing their food. Everyone liked them because they were such nice, loving people.[29] As time went on, some problems arose, but at their root the church was still a loving group of people.

My family and I have been in churches that would take care of you when you were sick or had a new baby or experienced some tragedy. And they were there when you had cause to celebrate: a wedding, an anniversary, a birthday, or graduation of a family member. They would take care of your children and would love them and would help you to teach them to love others. They were churches that did not see race or country of origin. They were like family to us, as the Bible calls them the family of God.[30]

---

26 John 13:35
27 Acts 2:42-47
28 Acts 4:32-35
29 Acts 2:42-47
30 1 Timothy 3:15

And we have been in churches who were just going through the Sunday routine then going about their own business the rest of the week, unaware and uncaring about whatever might be going on in the rest of the church. One of these churches is of God. The other is not.

So what are your options if you are to claim the offered prize of a loving "family"?

1. **Keep looking until you find one, no matter how far away it may be.**

The up side of this option is that once you have found it, the work is done. You have to help them maintain it. Some will attack it and try to change it, but you will have a lot of allies in keeping it loving and caring.

The down side is that the drive is not just a Sunday drive and maybe another, midweek, for a Bible study. If you are to be a part of a loving church, you need to be able to meet someone for coffee or lunch, stop by the hospital, take food by someone's house, get with someone to have a prayer together. These activities are almost impossible if the distance is too great.

We have lived at some distance from our church. It was a great time, living in the country with the four oldest of our kids. But we spent a lot of time in town. In our case four of the six of us worked in town and all four kids were in three different schools in town.

We started every day with a strategy session: Who would pick up whom, where and when; and what car would we leave where for someone to drive home when they were through working. I wouldn't trade that time for a house in the suburbs, but since we were always in town anyway, we didn't lose much in terms of church time. If the church is the only thing that is remote, it will be a different scene. You will be the absent one, and likely will never feel you have become a full-fledged part of the local church family.

2.   You can start a new one.

Starting something new is almost always fun. It is exciting to decide things like where and when you will meet, and to form new traditions and ways of accomplishing goals that God has set for the church.[31] You can figure out how you will become a known presence in your community and how you will use your collective influence for good. It will be an exhilarating time, one of forming close, lasting relationships with those who are working with you.

The problem with new things, though, is that in a fairly short period of time they become old things. My brother, Cecil, speaking of the worship service, once said that if you don't like traditions, and decide to do things differently every week, that will soon become your tradition. As new things become old,

31   "Prostitutes, Tax Collectors and You," David May, 2010, Chapter 8

they tend to be boring to those who are most excited about whatever is new.

There are a lot of problems with starting a new church, especially for someone without a lot of experience. Just from reading about the churches in the New Testament you can see that there are untold issues that can come up. You will need experienced guides, preferably right there with you.

You do not want to be divisive[32] so you will have to start the new church in such a way that it does not cause problems with existing churches. That may be difficult. But if you pull it off successfully, it will be a wonderful experience with a result worth telling about.

3.   Or you can stay with the one close by and try to change it.

This is the hardest option and the longest road to the goal. It will require patience and gentleness. It will require boldness and lots of love in unexpected places.

You will not get anywhere with this approach by being "in your face," or oppositional. You will have to start with things you have in common and build on them. You will have to lovingly confront unkind comments and actions taken toward others. And you will have to lead by example, having people over, setting up coffee meetings, starting ladies and

---

32   1 Corinthians 1:10

men's classes and discussion groups, showing up at the hospital and at home afterward, setting up times to serve the community, asking others to come along and persevering when it seems no one else has the time or the interest.[33] It will be a long haul, but it will work. Depending on your circumstance, this may be your best option.

4.   Or you can stay home.

This may be an attractive option.   There is a very active Facebook page that is kept up by Christians who are fed up with what they call "The Institutional Church."[34]   They call on Christians to leave all organized churches and band together in less formal groups.   But they don't ask you to go it alone.   They speak of the love and support you can still get from other Christians outside of the church organizations.

God doesn't want us to be hermits. Paul told the Corinthians that and said that even if you think you are not a part of the church, you still are.[35] As a hermit you would be cut off from all the benefits of the church. He built the church so we would not have to fight the fights in this life alone. We do not need to think that we are the only ones facing the problems of the world, just us and God. The church is here to

---

33   "Prostitutes, Tax Collectors and You," David May, 2010

34   www.facebook.com/ExposingTheInstitutionalChurch

35   1 Corinthians 12:14-20; Romans 12:8

remind us that we all have troubles. Whether they are sickness, or debts, or relationship issues, or something else, the church is here to help us find a way to hold up our heads and keep pushing on.[36]

And the church needs us. If we are not being a support to hurting Christians, we are neglecting our responsibility as God's ambassadors here on earth. Just as the Embassy's Office of the Consulate steps in to assist a citizen in trouble in a foreign country, so the church steps in when a citizen of heaven (that's us) gets in trouble here in this foreign land in which we live.[37]

So, we need the church and the church needs us. It may be a well-organized and faithful mega church with thousands of worshipers, or it may be a tiny home church meeting in someone's apartment. But as a Christian, you need to be a part of the church Jesus built. He built it for a purpose, to be his body here after his physical body rose up into the sky to go be with God. He intends for the church to continue the work he started here – worshipping God, training followers, spreading good news and helping those who need help. We cannot be as effective acting alone.

Choose an option, but don't let go of the dream of being the church that Jesus built.

---

36 Ecclesiastes 4:9-12
37 Romans 15:26-26

10

Promise #5: This World is Not Your Home

As the old song goes, "This world is not my home; I'm just a passing through. My treasures are laid up somewhere beyond the blue."[38] That is not just a songwriter's dream, it is a promise from God.[39]

How you view the world determines to a large extent how you react to it. And much of what we do and say in this life is in reaction to something. On a daily scale, we join in conversations. The nature of a conversation is that each participant is reacting to what the others have said. In traffic you are reacting to traffic signals and to the actions of other motorists. At home you react to your spouse's requests, to your kids' activities, and even to subtle signals.

If your view of the world is that money fixes most problems and hard work produces money, you are likely to be a hard worker. If you expect a bad outcome from whatever comes to you in this life, you will almost certainly not work too hard for a better

---

38 "This World is Not My Home" - Albert E Brumley, 1937
39 Hebrews 13:14

outcome. If you think everything is pre-determined and there is nothing we can do about it, you are not likely to be much of an activist about anything. If you think that evil forces are very powerful and the forces of good are weak, you may not take much action to try to overcome evil, thinking it would be futile. On the other hand, if you think that God is alive and active and is moving toward keeping his promises that good will triumph over evil, you will be more likely to want to join him in that work.

If we can look at the trouble in this world as another adventure in a long line of adventure stories, we are closer to claiming this promise. My wife, Charlene, and I have always been adventurers and it has led to a fun and exciting life. Our kids, and now our grandkids, love to hear and to retell the stories of our adventures. After we had our "perfect" family of three boys living in the woods out from Tallahassee, Florida, we adopted a seven year old foster child, a girl. After all the kids were grown and gone, we adopted an eleven year old foster child. Twice we moved from sunny Florida to frozen Minnesota in January. After we retired we home schooled two middle schoolers for a couple of years. When all the kids were gone again, we moved to Haiti to run a guest house. There are more stories that would take more space here than I want to give them, but my point is that we tend to get too focused on the potential, temporary outcomes of decisions we may make today. To borrow from a dated slogan, we need to make our decisions based on our informed view of what decision Jesus would make. He knew that some of his decisions would lead to his death, but he plowed on. He challenged what needed to be challenged and commended what needed to be commended. And though he did not have a place to lay his head,[40] I am thinking he slept well. He knew that this world is not his home.

Adopt a view that what is going on here and now is very temporary – short termed - and that our real home is in a place called forever. If we can do that, the "stuff of now" will take on much less importance in our lives. Lift up your eyes so that you see Jesus sitting on the right hand of God, watching us go through our daily lives and looking forward to the day we will join him there. Join him in the understanding that this world and whatever happens in it is not our home, and you will have a lot more fun here.

---

40   Luke 9:58

11

Where does
Jesus Come in?

What does Jesus have to do with it? This is where it gets a little complicated.

Jesus fulfills prophecy, forgives sin, and is really God in disguise.[41] We talk about Jesus being good news, and he is. But that's not what he called the good news. He spoke continually of the good news of the kingdom.[42] He kept saying the kingdom is near and the kingdom is at hand. [43] When he talked about why he came here, one the reasons was to bring the good news of the kingdom.[44]

Jesus of course is good news. You know the story. God needed a sacrifice for sin. You don't have to understand why. God is righteous and cannot tolerate being in the presence of unforgiven sin. We may not understand that. We just have to accept it. God had to have a perfect sacrifice and the only one available was his son, Jesus. Jesus was

41 John 14:7-9
42 Matthew 4:23
43 Mark 1:14-15
44 Luke 4:42-43

our sacrifice and brought the good news that we are forgiven, not because of what we have done, but because of what he did. We are not saved because of our good deeds, but so that we can do good deeds.[45] The Boy Scout motto is, "Do a good deed daily." A Boy Scout is not a Boy Scout because he does good deeds; he does good deeds because he is a Boy Scout.

That's where the kingdom comes in. Some people say the kingdom of God is the church and they are partly right. But the kingdom of God is much bigger than that and it is good news. God's kingdom is his rule over the hearts of good people. The good people will be in the kingdom and the bad people will be out.[46] Jesus talks incessantly about it. He tells stories about it, about how hard it is for a rich man to get in,[47] how valuable it is, who will be in it and who will be out, what it will be like. He starts many of his stories with the words, "The kingdom of God is like..." He really wants us to understand it.

It is like a man who found a very expensive pearl, went and sold all he had and bought it. Or like a man who found a treasure in a field, sold all he had and bought the field.[48] In both those

45 Ephesians 2:8-10
46 Matthew 25:31-46
47 Luke 18:25
48 Matthew 13:44-46

analogies, at the end of the story, the man had the kingdom - and nothing else. They both sold everything they had to gain the kingdom. That is its value.

And in a couple of the stories, there is some sorting going on. There is the man whose enemy sowed weeds in his field. The servants wanted to pull them out, but in the interest of accuracy he told his guys to wait until the harvest. Then they would sort it all out and burn the weeds.[49] In a similar story some fishermen sorted out fish at the end of the day, keeping the good and discarding the bad.[50] When he explained the story, Jesus said that at the end of time the angels would come and separate the "evil" people from the "Godly" people. Note the distinction. He didn't mention the people who got part of their worship wrong or those who got it all right. He said nothing of those who made mistakes in their relationships, or who may have had their priorities askew. What he did say, though, was evil people and Godly people. Godly people are those who love God and want to act like he wants them to act. Evil people don't, even if they are evil religious people.

And that is good news. It is good news if you are willing to accept God's promises, to drop your

---

49 Matthew 13:24-30

50 Matthew 13:47-50

loyalties to the things and people of the world, and to act the way he wants you to act. Acting that way will make you loving, gentle, kind and peaceful, among other things.[51] It is not likely to make you rich.

---

51 Galatians 5:19-23

12
What's the Catch?

You are right, there is a bit of a catch. Though, it's not so much a catch as it is a condition. The writer of the well known little song, "Jesus Loves Me," understood that condition. The second verse goes: "Jesus loves me! He will stay close beside me all the way. Thou hast bled and died for me; I will henceforth live for thee."[52]

That's the tradeoff. He died for us; we live for him. But it really isn't hard when you understand the magnitude of the prize.

This is not like "If you buy our magazine, we will put your name in the pot for the drawing for the luxury car." This is a solid promise, tit for tat, from someone who has always kept his promises. And the reward is forever.

Forever is a hard idea to get your head around. The last verse of "Amazing Grace" explains it to me better than anything else I have heard, "When we've been there ten thousand years, bright, shining as

---

52 "Jesus Love Me," Anna Bartlett Warner. 1860. However there are many variations of verses and the one listed here was likely added later.

the sun, we've no less days to sing God's praise than when we'd first begun."[53]

You see, we spend most of our lives trying to figure out how we will get the most out of this life. We want to see all the sights, experience all the experiences, do everything fun there is to do.

But Jesus says to drop all that stuff and just follow him. He will make it worth your while. He is the only one in the Bible who gives a detailed description of the judgment. Others say we will be judged by what we do, but Jesus takes it a step further.[54] Jesus uses a metaphor as he often does to describe important things. He talks about the judge separating sheep from goats. The difference is simple. It is that the good guys, the sheep, helped people who needed help. The bad guys, the goats, didn't. At the end of Jesus' illustration, the good guys go off for their forever reward. The goats don't. That's pretty straightforward. Today church leaders will often give a lot of logical reasons not to help people. And Jesus says that at the judgment those who did not help will be punished.

Even the details are not hard, unless you are just someone who insists on doing things your own way. After Jesus went home, leaving his students here to carry on his work, the Holy Spirit assembled

53 "Amazing Grace," John Newton, 1779. Final verse added by Harriet Beecher Stow
54 Matthew 25:31-46

a crowd in Jerusalem. There were several thousand of them. Peter stood up and preached a convicting sermon; so much so that the crowd was touched and asked him what they should do. His answer was, again, very straightforward: repent (be sorry and change your ways) and be baptized (buried in water). Where we go wrong in trying to follow instructions like that is in trying to make sense of them. Like the counselor told our son over and over, "No questions, just do it." It's a hard lesson.

Judgment

Yes there will be a judgment, but it does not have to be a scary thing. Isaiah 40:9 says to the people of Israel, "You have good news to tell." He says it three times in a short verse with only 43 words in it. It is good news, and the good news is, "Here is your God." Why would that be good news if God had come to punish them? It wouldn't.

Isaiah goes on to say that God is coming to bring his reward. And this in not like the "rewards" you get online where you have to fill out all these forms and the reward turns out to be 2% off a humongous purchase you have to make. God has his reward in his hand.[55]

Isaiah says that God takes care of his people. Then he goes on to talk about how big and powerful

---

55 Isaiah 40:10

God is. God can keep his promises. He compares God to the armies, navies and air forces of all the nations put together and says the nations are like dust on God's measuring scales. That's the good news. God will take care of you and he is able. He does not become tired or need to rest.[56] Children become tired and need to rest; young people trip and fall. But the people who trust the Lord will rise up like the eagle; they will run and not need rest; they will walk and not be tired.[57]

People who love God have a different view of the world. Being tired is a blessing. Being strained is a gift from God. Whatever happens in this world stays in this world. It is temporary – short term temporary when you look at time the way God does. And that changes everything.

God's promise is of a place with metaphorical gold streets, with a stream flowing though it with no pesticides or fertilizers, where there are no tears - that is, there is no reason to cry, not that your tear ducts get stopped up. There is no death there. For Disney lovers it is like a forever Disneyworld with a new theme park every day, and your feet don't hurt.

There will be people who miss out on it, but that will be because they rejected the promises. There is no good reason for a reasonable person to

56 Isaiah 40:28
57 Isaiah 40:30-31

turn down the promise that God will give you freedom from worry, freedom from being afraid of anything, freedom from death, and a Disney trip that
will last forever.

13

Good News?

Yes, there is good news. There is a God, and that is good news. If there were not a creator God, this life would be all there is and, at least for most of us, that would be exceedingly sad. This life with all its disappointments, all its decisions with no good answers, all its betrayals and pains would be the whole story. It would be like an unfinished movie that left all the good guys pinned down behind the overturned wagon and killed them off before the cavalry arrived.

But the cavalry is coming and it will get here on time.[58] Jesus is coming back and that is good news. It need only be scary to those who have refused to see it his way – to those who have chosen the temporary things of this world with all its pains and sorrows over the bright promises of the creator.[59]

The Church

And in the meantime Jesus' church is good news. He said over and over that his people should

---

58 "A Call to Arms, Out of the Pews and Into the Streets," Chapter 6: "Trumpets and Drums" by David May

59 2 Peter 1:5-11

be telling other people about the good news that the kingdom is at hand. The church is good news because that is where we find encouragement. It is good news because it teaches us and others about how Jesus lived and how he wants us to live. It is where we find people who truly love us, who will put our interests ahead of their own, and where we can practice our love for others, per Jesus' instructions. And it will lead us home.

ABOUT THE AUTHOR

David May lives is Port au Prince Haiti where he and his wife, Charlene, are the hosts for a guest house serving medical teams and others coming from the states to help the people of Haiti. He has written three other books which can be found at amazon.com/author/davidmay

Made in the USA
San Bernardino, CA
27 September 2015